Summary

1.

2.

3.

4.

      a.

      b.

      c.

      d.

      e.

      f.

      g.

      h.

      i.

      j.

      k.

      l.

      m.

      n.

      o.

      p.

      q.

      r.

      s.

      t.

rumble.com
How a Video Sharing Platform Changed the Game

Marc Ferrari

rumble.com:
How a Video Charing Platform Changed the Game
Copyright © 2023 by Marc Ferrari
All rights reserved.

"Rumble is creating the rails to a new infrastructure that will not be bullied by cancel culture. We are a movement that does not stifle, censor, or punish creativity and freedom of expression."

Chris Pavlovski
Rumble.com founder and CEO

rumble.com: How a Video Sharing Platform is Changing the Game

The Birth of Rumble.com:
Founding and Early Development

The story of how Rumble.com came to be is an interesting one that speaks to the creativity and determination of its founder and CEO, Chris Pavlovski, a Canadian entrepreneur. Born in 1978 in Toronto, Pavlovski grew up in a family of entrepreneurs and gained an early appreciation for hard work and innovation. After completing high school, he attended the University of Windsor in Ontario, where he studied business.

After graduating, Pavlovski worked in the tech industry for a number of years, gaining valuable experience in software development, digital marketing, and sales. In 2008, he founded his first company, which provided online marketing solutions for small businesses. However, it wasn't until he founded Rumble.com in 2013 that Pavlovski truly hit his stride as an entrepreneur.

The idea for Rumble.com came to Pavlovski as a response to what he saw as a problem with the existing video sharing platforms. YouTube, which had long been the dominant player in the market, was increasingly seen as censoring content that did not align with its political or ideological views. Pavlovski saw an opportunity to create a platform that would be more open to free speech and independent content creators.

The platform was founded on the principles of free speech, fair use, and independent journalism. From the beginning,

Rumble.com aimed to provide a platform for all voices, regardless of political affiliation, gender, race, or religion.

Under Pavlovski's leadership, Rumble.com has grown rapidly, attracting millions of users and establishing itself as a major player in the video sharing market. In 2021, the platform reported that it had over 120 million monthly active users and had paid out over $40 million in earnings to its creators.

Pavlovski's success with Rumble.com has not gone unnoticed. In 2021, he was named one of Canada's Top 40 Under 40, a prestigious award that recognizes outstanding achievement by young leaders in business, innovation, and community service. He has also been interviewed by major news outlets, including Fox News and The Wall Street Journal, and has become a popular figure among conservative media personalities.

While Rumble.com has not been without its controversies, Pavlovski has remained committed to his vision of providing a platform for free speech and independent journalism. He has been outspoken in his support of content creators and has worked to ensure that Rumble.com remains a welcoming and inclusive community for all users.

Back in 2013, Pavlovski had a successful video services company, but he realized that many of his clients struggled to get their content seen by a larger audience. So he had an idea - what if there was a platform where anyone could upload and share their videos with the world? That was the beginning of Rumble.com.

In its early days, Rumble.com was a small operation with only a handful of employees. But despite its size, Pavlovski had big ambitions for the site. He knew that in order to compete with YouTube, which was then and still is the dominant video sharing platform, Rumble.com would have to offer something different.

One of Rumble.com's early advantages was its focus on monetization. At the time, YouTube had a reputation for being difficult to make money on, and many creators were frustrated by the low payouts they received from the platform. Rumble.com offered a revenue sharing model that allowed creators to earn a share of the advertising revenue generated by their videos. This was a major selling point for creators who were looking for a platform that would allow them to make a living from their content.

Another key feature of Rumble.com's early development was its focus on quality. Pavlovski believed that in order to compete with YouTube, Rumble.com needed to offer a superior viewing experience. To that end, the site prioritized high-quality video and audio, as well as an intuitive and user-friendly interface. This attention to detail helped Rumble.com stand out from the crowd and win over users who were tired of the clunky interfaces and low-quality video that were common on other platforms.

Rumble.com also made a conscious effort to differentiate itself from YouTube in other ways. For example, the site positioned itself as a defender of free speech, and made it clear that it would not censor content unless it violated Canadian law. This stance won the site praise from some creators who felt that YouTube was becoming too restrictive.

As Rumble.com grew, it faced a number of challenges. One of the biggest was the difficulty of attracting users away from YouTube, which had an enormous user base and a near-monopoly on the video sharing market. Additionally, the site faced criticism from some quarters over its monetization policies, with some creators arguing that they were not earning enough money from their videos.

Despite these challenges, Rumble.com continued to grow, and by 2021 it had become a significant player in the video sharing space. The site had attracted a large and active community of creators, and was generating significant revenue from advertising. Today, Rumble.com is considered one of the top alternatives to YouTube, and is widely seen as a promising up-and-comer in the video sharing world.

Looking back, it's clear that Rumble.com's success is due in large part to its focus on quality, monetization, and user experience. By offering a platform that was designed specifically for creators, and by prioritizing the things that mattered most to them, Rumble.com was able to carve out a niche for itself in a highly competitive market. And while it still has a long way to go to catch up to YouTube, there's no doubt that Rumble.com has made a significant impact on the world of online video sharing.

The Rumble.com Mission:
Providing a Platform for Free Speech and Content Creators

Rumble.com's mission to provide a platform for free speech and content creators has been a driving force behind the site since its inception. The founder recognized early on that there was a need for a platform that allowed all voices to be heard, without censorship or bias. This commitment to free speech and fairness has helped Rumble.com stand out in a crowded field of video sharing platforms.

One of the key ways that Rumble.com has advanced its mission of free speech is by taking a more relaxed approach to content moderation than many other platforms. While some sites have been criticized for heavy-handed or opaque content moderation policies, Rumble.com has sought to strike a balance between allowing free expression and enforcing community standards. The site only removes content that is illegal under Canadian law or that violates its community guidelines, which has earned it praise from some creators who feel that other platforms are becoming too restrictive.

Rumble.com is also dedicated to providing a platform that is friendly to all viewpoints. Unlike some other sites that have been accused of bias against certain political viewpoints, Rumble.com is committed to allowing all voices to be heard. This inclusivity has made the site popular among creators who feel that they are being silenced or marginalized on other platforms.

In addition to its commitment to free speech, Rumble.com is also dedicated to providing a platform that is fair and transparent for content creators. The site's revenue sharing model ensures that creators are fairly compensated for their work, and the site is committed to providing analytics and other tools that help creators understand how their content is performing. This commitment to transparency and fairness has helped build a loyal community of creators who trust and value the Rumble.com platform.

The success of Rumble.com's mission to provide a platform for free speech and content creators can be seen in the diverse and vibrant community of creators that the site has attracted. From political commentators to musicians, comedians to educational channels, Rumble.com has become a hub for a wide range of content creators. And as the site continues to grow and evolve, its commitment to free speech and fairness will remain at the core of its mission, driving the site's success and attracting new creators to the platform.

Building a Strong Foundation:
The Infrastructure of rumble.com

Sure thing! Rumble.com's infrastructure is a critical aspect of the platform that ensures that it can handle large volumes of traffic while providing a smooth, fast, and secure user experience. In this chapter, we'll take a closer look at the different components that make up Rumble.com's infrastructure and how they work together to keep the platform running smoothly.

Firstly, Rumble.com's cloud-based architecture is the foundation of the platform's infrastructure. It was built on top of Amazon Web Services (AWS), which is a cloud-based service that provides a range of tools and services for running applications and hosting websites, but they have decided to invest in their own cloud infrastructure so that their business can carry on independently of other companies like Amazon, who owns AWS.

Rumble.com also uses a Content Delivery Network (CDN) to ensure that videos are delivered to users quickly and efficiently. A CDN is a network of servers located all over the world, which allows the platform to deliver content from the server closest to the user. This helps to reduce latency and improve the user experience, particularly for users who are located in different parts of the world.

The platform also has a range of security measures in place to protect its infrastructure and user data. These measures include industry-standard encryption protocols, firewalls, and other security tools that help to prevent unauthorized access and protect user data from cyber threats. Rumble.com also uses monitoring tools to detect and prevent attacks, ensuring that the platform remains secure and reliable.

In terms of the software infrastructure, Rumble.com uses a range of tools and technologies to ensure that the platform is fast, responsive, and user-friendly. The front-end is built using modern frameworks such as React and AngularJS, which provide a responsive and intuitive user interface. The back-end uses a range of technologies, including Node.js, Python, and Ruby on Rails, which provide a powerful and flexible infrastructure for handling user requests and serving video content. The platform also uses a range of data storage technologies, including both relational and NoSQL databases, to store user data and video content.

Overall, Rumble.com's infrastructure is a complex and sophisticated system that allows the platform to provide a fast, reliable, and secure experience for users. The cloud-based architecture, CDN, and security measures all work together to ensure that the platform can handle large volumes of traffic and protect user data from cyber threats. The use of modern front-end and back-end technologies and data storage technologies ensures that the platform is responsive and user-friendly. As Rumble.com continues to grow and attract more users, its infrastructure will continue to evolve, providing an even better user experience for content creators and viewers alike.

Rumble.com's User-Friendly Interface: Design and Features

Rumble.com's user-friendly interface is one of the defining features of the platform. From the moment you arrive on the site, it's clear that a lot of thought and care has gone into creating a design that is both aesthetically pleasing and highly functional.

The site's homepage is clean and simple, with a minimalistic design that prioritizes ease of use. The search bar is prominently displayed at the top of the page, making it easy to find the content you're looking for. The categories for browsing content, popular channels, and trending videos are also prominently displayed, allowing users to quickly and easily discover new content.

One of the most impressive features of Rumble.com's interface is its video player. The player is highly customizable, allowing users to adjust the video quality, speed, and captions. It also has options for standard and full-screen views, making it easy to watch videos on a variety of devices. The player is optimized for fast loading times, even on slower internet connections, ensuring that users can enjoy their favorite videos without frustrating buffering.

Uploading content to Rumble.com is also incredibly easy, thanks to the site's intuitive content management system. Creators can quickly and easily add titles, descriptions, and tags to their videos, making it easier for users to discover their content. The site also offers a variety of monetization options for creators, including advertising, sponsorships, and tips from fans, making it an attractive platform for content creators of all types.

But perhaps one of the most compelling aspects of Rumble.com's interface is its community features. The site places a strong emphasis on community, encouraging users to engage with each other and with content creators through comments, likes, and shares. The site also features a messaging system for direct communication, making it easy for users to connect with each other and with the creators they admire.

Overall, Rumble.com's user-friendly interface is a major selling point for the platform. By prioritizing ease of use and engagement, the site has created a platform that is accessible and enjoyable for both creators and viewers. And as the site continues to grow and evolve, its user-friendly design and features will no doubt continue to be a key factor in its success.

Rumble.com vs. YouTube: Competing for Market Share

The competition between Rumble.com and YouTube has been one of the most exciting developments in the video sharing market in recent years. While YouTube has long been the dominant player, Rumble.com has been making significant strides in the industry, with a focus on professional content creators and a commitment to free speech.

One of the key differences between the two platforms is their focus. YouTube has traditionally been a platform for user-generated content, with a massive user base and a wide variety of content ranging from vlogs and DIY tutorials to music videos and short films. In contrast, Rumble.com has been more focused on professional content creators, including media companies and production studios. This has allowed the platform to attract high-profile content creators, such as Fox News and The Epoch Times, which has helped to increase its visibility and attract a wider user base.

Another difference between the two platforms is their approach to monetization. YouTube has a more established monetization system, with creators earning revenue through ads, sponsorships, and partnerships. However, YouTube has faced criticism for its monetization policies, which have been seen as inconsistent and overly restrictive. In contrast, Rumble.com has taken a more flexible approach to monetization, offering a variety of options for content creators, including advertising, sponsorships, and tips from fans. This has allowed creators to more effectively monetize their content and earn a living from their work.

Both platforms also place a strong emphasis on user engagement and community building. Both Rumble.com and YouTube have features that allow users to like, comment, and share videos, and both platforms encourage users to engage with content creators and each other. This has helped to create vibrant and supportive communities on both platforms, which has in turn helped to drive growth and increase user engagement.

However, both platforms have also faced their fair share of controversies. YouTube has come under fire for issues related to content moderation and demonetization, with many creators feeling that the platform's policies are overly restrictive and inconsistent. Rumble.com has also faced criticism for its approach to copyright infringement, with some creators claiming that the platform does not do enough to protect their intellectual property.

Despite these challenges, the competition between Rumble.com and YouTube is driving innovation and growth in the video sharing market. As Rumble.com continues to expand its user base and attract high-profile content creators, it is becoming an increasingly serious competitor to YouTube. And with its focus on free speech, flexible monetization options, and commitment to community building, Rumble.com is well-positioned to continue to compete with YouTube for market share in the years to come.

Overall, the competition between Rumble.com and YouTube is an exciting development for the video sharing market, and is likely to lead to continued growth and innovation in the industry. While both platforms have their strengths and weaknesses, the competition between them is ultimately good for users and content creators alike, as it encourages both platforms to continually improve and evolve.

The Unique Rumble.com Revenue Model: Creator-Focused Monetization

Rumble.com's creator-focused revenue model has been a significant factor in the platform's success. Unlike other video-sharing platforms, Rumble.com allows content creators to earn revenue directly from their content, giving them a greater sense of ownership and control over their work. This approach has attracted many content creators to the platform, as they appreciate the platform's emphasis on supporting creators and their ability to earn a fair share of revenue from their work.

One of the most significant advantages of Rumble.com's monetization system is its ad revenue sharing model. When an advertisement is displayed on a video, Rumble.com splits the revenue generated from the ad between the platform and the content creator. This is different from other platforms, where the platform often takes a larger percentage of the ad revenue, leaving content creators with only a small share. With Rumble.com, content creators are incentivized to create high-quality content that attracts viewers and generates ad revenue, as they can earn a larger share of the revenue from their work.

Rumble.com also provides additional revenue streams for content creators through its licensing program. The platform allows content creators to license their work for use in other media, such as news broadcasts or television shows. This can be a significant revenue source for content creators, particularly if their work goes viral or becomes particularly popular. Rumble.com's licensing program allows creators to set their own licensing fees, giving them more control over how their content is used and how much they earn from it.

The platform also offers a creator support team, which provides guidance and support for content creators looking to maximize their revenue potential. The team helps creators to understand the platform's monetization features, provides guidance on content creation and distribution, and assists with content promotion to help creators grow their audience and reach more viewers. This level of support is particularly valuable for new creators who may be unsure of how to monetize their content effectively.

In comparison to other video-sharing platforms, Rumble.com's monetization system provides significant advantages for content creators. The ad revenue sharing model allows creators to earn a larger share of revenue from their content, while the licensing program provides additional revenue streams. The creator support team is also a unique feature that sets the platform apart from others, as it provides personalized support and guidance to help content creators succeed on the platform.

Rumble.com's creator-focused revenue model has been a significant factor in the platform's growth and success. The ad revenue sharing model, licensing program, and creator support team all help to provide content creators with more opportunities to monetize their content and earn a fair share of revenue. As the platform continues to grow and attract more content creators, it is likely that Rumble.com's monetization model will continue to be a major factor in its continued success.

Rumble.com's Algorithm and Recommendations: Promoting Viral Videos

Rumble.com's algorithm and recommendation system are key features of the platform that have helped it become a popular and successful video-sharing site. The algorithm is designed to promote videos that are likely to be popular with users, while also helping to ensure that a diverse range of content creators can succeed on the platform.

The algorithm is based on several factors, including a user's viewing history, likes and dislikes, and other interactions with the platform. This information is then used to make personalized recommendations to users, suggesting videos that they are likely to find interesting and engaging.

Rumble.com's algorithm is different from those used by other platforms in that it prioritizes smaller content creators. While other platforms may focus on larger, more established creators, Rumble.com's algorithm is designed to promote a diverse range of creators, including those who may not have a large following yet. This approach helps to create a more level playing field, and it gives new and emerging creators a chance to reach a wider audience.

In addition to the algorithm, Rumble.com also provides tools to help content creators optimize their videos for the platform. For example, creators can add tags and descriptions to their videos, which help the algorithm better understand the content and improve its chances of being recommended to users. The platform also provides analytics tools that allow creators to track the performance of their videos and make adjustments as needed to improve their visibility and engagement.

One of the unique features of Rumble.com's recommendation system is the use of human curation. While the algorithm plays a significant role in recommending videos to users, Rumble.com also employs a team of curators who manually review and select videos to be featured on the platform's homepage and in other prominent positions. This approach helps to ensure that viewers are presented with high-quality content that is relevant and engaging.

Overall, Rumble.com's algorithm and recommendation system are critical factors in the platform's success. By promoting a diverse range of content creators and providing tools to optimize content for the algorithm, the platform has created a supportive environment for creators to thrive. The use of human curation also helps to ensure that viewers are presented with high-quality content that is relevant to their interests. As the platform continues to grow and evolve, it is likely that its algorithm and recommendation system will continue to play a critical role in promoting viral videos and helping content creators reach   new   audiences.

Community Management:
Policies and Enforcement

Rumble.com has implemented a set of community management policies and guidelines to ensure that its platform is a safe and positive space for all users. The platform's commitment to community management is critical to maintaining user trust and encouraging continued engagement on the platform.

The platform's policies cover a wide range of topics, including prohibited content and acceptable behavior. Rumble.com has a zero-tolerance policy for content that promotes violence, hate speech, harassment, or illegal activities. Users who violate these policies may have their content removed, their accounts suspended, or may even be banned from the platform entirely. These measures ensure that the platform is a safe and welcoming space for all users.

To enforce these policies, Rumble.com has a team of moderators who review content and user reports to identify and address any violations. The platform also provides users with the ability to report any content that they feel is in violation of the platform's policies. These reports are reviewed by the moderation team, and appropriate action is taken as necessary.

Rumble.com's community management policies also extend to its monetization features. The platform has strict guidelines for what types of content are eligible for monetization, and users who violate these guidelines may have their monetization privileges revoked. Additionally, the platform has guidelines for sponsored content, which must be clearly labeled and comply with all applicable laws and regulations.

In addition to enforcing its policies, Rumble.com takes an active role in promoting a positive community culture. The platform encourages users to engage with each other in respectful and constructive ways and provides tools to help users manage their interactions. For example, users can block or mute other users if they feel that they are being harassed or targeted. These features help to ensure that all users feel comfortable and respected while using the platform.

Rumble.com's commitment to community management is a critical aspect of its success. By providing a safe and positive space for users to engage with each other, the platform encourages continued engagement and fosters a strong sense of community. As the platform continues to grow and evolve, its community management policies and enforcement measures will remain essential to maintaining a positive and welcoming environment for all users.

Rumble.com's Impact on Online Video Sharing: A Historical Perspective

Rumble.com's impact on the online video sharing industry cannot be overstated. Before Rumble.com's arrival, many creators faced significant challenges when it came to monetizing their content. YouTube's strict policies around monetization made it difficult for creators to earn a living from their content, leading many to turn to alternative platforms that offered more flexible monetization models.

This is where Rumble.com came in. The platform was founded on the principle of providing a more creator-friendly monetization model that allowed creators to earn money from their content in new and innovative ways. This unique revenue model, combined with Rumble.com's commitment to free speech and its user-friendly interface, quickly attracted a following and sparked a significant shift in the online video sharing landscape.

As Rumble.com grew in popularity, other platforms began to take notice, and many started to adopt similar monetization models and policies. This competition fueled innovation in the industry, leading to the development of new features and tools that made it easier for creators to share and monetize their content.

Rumble.com's impact on the industry can also be seen in the way it has given a voice to creators from all walks of life. Many creators who might otherwise have been unable to share their content with a wider audience have found a home on Rumble.com. This has resulted in a more diverse and vibrant online ecosystem, with creators from all over the world sharing their perspectives and experiences.

In addition to its impact on the online video sharing industry, Rumble.com has also had a broader cultural impact. By giving a voice to creators who might otherwise have been overlooked, the platform has helped to foster a more inclusive and democratic online culture.

Overall, Rumble.com's impact on the online video sharing industry has been significant, and the platform continues to push the boundaries of what is possible in the industry. As it continues to grow and evolve, it will undoubtedly continue to shape the online video landscape for years to come.

Case Studies:
Creators Who Found Success on rumble.com

Rumble.com has been a home for a diverse range of creators, providing them with an opportunity to showcase their talents and grow their audiences. The platform has become a hub for creators who are looking for a more user-friendly and equitable platform to monetize their content.

One of the earliest and most notable success stories on Rumble.com is that of Tim Pool. He is a political commentator and journalist who quickly established himself as a major presence on the platform. He has been able to earn a significant income from his content, leveraging Rumble.com's unique monetization model. Pool's approach to political commentary, which often incorporates on-the-ground reporting, has resonated with Rumble.com users, and he has built a large following on the platform.

Another creator who has found great success on Rumble.com is Gavin McInnes, the Canadian filmmaker and comedian. McInnes, who co-founded Vice Media, used Rumble.com to launch a new career as a political commentator and comedian. His irreverent, often controversial, style has resonated with many Rumble.com users, and he has been able to build a successful brand on the platform.

Ify Yani, a Nigerian chef and food blogger, is another creator who has found great success on Rumble.com. Her videos, which showcase traditional Nigerian cooking techniques and ingredients, have been a hit with Rumble.com users, and she has been able to build a successful brand around her content. Yani had struggled to gain traction on YouTube, but found a more engaged and diverse audience on Rumble.com, which has helped her to achieve her goals as a creator.

These success stories are a testament to Rumble.com's commitment to providing a platform that is focused on free speech and diversity. By providing a more creator-friendly monetization model and a platform that promotes virality, Rumble.com has become a hub for creators who are looking to build a career in the online video space.

Rumble.com's success in attracting and supporting a diverse range of creators has disrupted the online video industry and has challenged the dominance of platforms such as YouTube. The platform's user-friendly interface, unique monetization model, and commitment to free speech have made it an attractive alternative to other video-sharing platforms.

As more and more creators discover the benefits of Rumble.com, the platform is poised to continue to disrupt the industry and provide a space for creators to build their brands, reach a wider audience, and achieve their goals.

Viral Videos:
Examining the Characteristics of Popular Rumble.com Content

Viral videos have always been an important aspect of online video sharing, and Rumble.com is no exception. In fact, Rumble.com has placed a strong emphasis on promoting viral videos, as it can lead to increased revenue and exposure for creators on the platform.

There are certain characteristics that are often present in viral videos on Rumble.com. These videos tend to be highly engaging, often featuring compelling stories or unique perspectives that resonate with viewers. They may also tap into a larger cultural moment or trend, which can help to create a sense of community around the video.

In addition to the creative elements, viral videos on Rumble.com also tend to be visually stunning, with unique imagery or high production values. The use of professional-level editing and sound design can help to create a more polished final product, which is more likely to capture the viewer's attention.

While the creative elements are important, it is also important for creators to promote their videos effectively. This may involve leveraging social media or other online channels to drive traffic to the video, or engaging with the audience in the comments section to build a sense of community around the content.

Creators who are able to tap into these characteristics and promote their content effectively are often able to achieve viral success on Rumble.com. This success can lead to increased revenue and exposure for the creator, as well as greater visibility for their message or brand.

One of the benefits of Rumble.com's algorithm is that it is designed to promote videos that are likely to go viral. This means that creators who are able to create content that aligns with the characteristics of viral videos on the platform are more likely to be promoted to a wider audience.

Viral videos are an important aspect of Rumble.com, and there are certain characteristics that are often present in successful videos on the platform. By creating visually stunning and engaging content, and promoting it effectively, creators can increase their chances of achieving viral success on Rumble.com. As the platform continues to grow and evolve, viral videos will continue to be a key element of its success.

Controversies and Criticisms: Rumble.com's Reputation and Response

Rumble.com, like any large online platform, has faced its fair share of controversies and criticisms. However, the company has been proactive in addressing these issues and ensuring that the platform remains a trusted and valuable resource for creators and users alike.

One of the most common criticisms of Rumble.com has been allegations of biased content moderation. Some creators have claimed that their videos were unfairly removed or demonetized due to political or ideological differences with Rumble.com's leadership. In response to these concerns, Rumble.com has emphasized its commitment to providing a platform for free speech and open dialogue, regardless of political or ideological viewpoints. The company has also made efforts to improve transparency in its content moderation policies and has developed a robust appeals process for creators who believe their content was removed unfairly.

Another area of controversy has been Rumble.com's revenue-sharing model. Some creators have expressed frustration over the percentage of revenue that Rumble.com takes from their content, which they believe is too high. In response to these concerns, Rumble.com has emphasized its creator-focused approach to revenue sharing, which is designed to provide fair compensation for creators while also allowing the platform to sustain itself. The company has also implemented new features to help creators earn more revenue, such as a tipping system and a merchandising platform.

In addition to these concerns, Rumble.com has also faced criticism over its handling of user data and privacy. Some users have expressed concern that their personal information is not adequately protected, and that Rumble.com's data collection practices are too invasive. In response to these concerns, Rumble.com has emphasized its commitment to protecting user data and privacy, and has implemented a range of measures to safeguard user information. These measures include strict data retention policies, encryption of user data, and regular audits of the platform's security practices.

Despite these controversies and criticisms, Rumble.com has maintained a strong reputation among many creators and users. The platform's commitment to free speech and open dialogue has resonated with many who are looking for an alternative to more traditional social media platforms, and the platform's creator-focused revenue-sharing model has provided a viable source of income for many content creators. Rumble.com has also been recognized for its user-friendly interface and advanced algorithm, which help promote viral content and provide a more personalized user experience.

As Rumble.com continues to grow and evolve, it will undoubtedly face additional controversies and criticisms. However, the company's response to these concerns will be critical in maintaining the platform's reputation and user base. By remaining transparent and responsive to user feedback, Rumble.com can continue to provide a valuable platform for creators and users alike, and help shape the future of online video sharing.

Expanding Horizons:
Rumble.com's International Growth

Rumble.com, a video sharing platform that began in Canada, has been making waves in the online content creation industry since its inception. As it gained popularity in North America, the team behind Rumble.com decided to expand its horizons and make its services available to a global audience.

To make this happen, Rumble.com forged partnerships with international media companies and influencers to promote its brand and reach a wider audience. In addition, it created tools and features to help creators from different countries to upload and share their content on the platform.

One major initiative Rumble.com undertook to support international growth was the addition of multi-language support. With this feature, users can now view the website and the videos in their preferred language, which makes the platform more accessible and user-friendly for non-English speakers.

Rumble.com also created a monetization program to incentivize content creators to upload videos in their local languages. By doing so, they can reach a broader audience and potentially earn more revenue from their content. The program was particularly helpful for creators in countries where there were few opportunities for monetizing online content, providing them with an alternative revenue stream.

Rumble.com's international expansion hasn't been without its challenges, however. The company had to navigate various regulations and restrictions related to online content in different countries. It also faced competition from established video sharing platforms in some regions.

Despite these challenges, Rumble.com has continued to make progress in its global expansion efforts. Its user base has grown, and the platform has become a significant player in the online video sharing market. As it continues to evolve and expand, Rumble.com's impact on the online content creation industry is sure to be felt for years to come.

Partnerships and Collaborations: Rumble.com's Strategy for Expansion

Rumble.com's mission to provide a free and open video sharing platform for content creators and their audiences has been a driving force behind the platform's success. The company's commitment to collaboration and partnerships has also played a vital role in its growth and expansion.

In order to increase its reach and impact, Rumble.com has developed strategic partnerships with a number of other companies, media outlets, and individuals. By leveraging the strengths of these partners, Rumble.com has been able to enhance its capabilities, expand its user base, and diversify its content offerings.

One example of Rumble.com's successful partnership strategy is its collaboration with Newsmax, a leading conservative news and media organization. In 2020, Rumble.com and Newsmax announced a strategic partnership that would allow Rumble.com videos to be featured on Newsmax's online platforms, reaching a wider audience of conservative news consumers.

This partnership not only increased the visibility of Rumble.com's content, but it also allowed Newsmax to diversify its video offerings, attracting a new audience to its platform. By leveraging the strengths of both organizations, this partnership was a win-win for both Rumble.com and Newsmax.

Another example of Rumble.com's successful partnership strategy is its collaboration with Parler, a social media platform that emphasizes free speech and conservative values. In the aftermath of the 2020 U.S. presidential election, Parler was removed from major app stores and faced other challenges related to content moderation.

Rumble.com saw an opportunity to collaborate with Parler, offering its platform as a video hosting solution for Parler's content creators. This partnership helped Rumble.com to expand its user base, while also providing Parler with a much-needed alternative to other video hosting services.

Other notable partnerships that have contributed to Rumble.com's growth and expansion include its collaboration with The Epoch Times, a conservative news outlet, and its partnership with Michael Malice, a political commentator and author. These partnerships have allowed Rumble.com to diversify its content offerings and expand its user base, while also providing its partners with access to a new audience and distribution platform.

Rumble acquisition of locals.com

Rumble.com has a good partnership with Locals.com, a social network that allows content creators to monetize their content and engage with their communities. This partnership was a significant move for both companies and has the potential to reshape the way content creators operate in the online space.

Locals.com was founded by Dave Rubin, a well-known political commentator and comedian, and has gained popularity among creators who feel that existing social media platforms like Facebook and Twitter are not conducive to free speech. The platform allows creators to have full control over their content, including their own branding, pricing, and subscription models. It also offers tools for creators to build their own communities and interact with their fans directly.

Rumble.com's partnership with Locals.com was a strategic move that aligns with their core mission of empowering content creators.

In order to strength the platform, in October 2021 rumble.com has reached an agreement to acquire locals.com.

By integrating with Locals.com, Rumble.com aims to provide more monetization options for creators and expand their reach to a wider audience. The acquisition will enable creators on Rumble.com to create private subscription-based content, which can be shared with their fans on Locals.com.

The acquisition also benefits Locals.com by providing them with a vast library of videos from Rumble.com, which they can use to further engage with their users. The agreement allows Locals.com to showcase Rumble.com's video content on their platform, providing users with a wider range of content to explore.

Overall, this acquisition represents a shift in the way that content creators can monetize their work and engage with their fans. By working together, the two platforms offer creators a unique opportunity to build their brand and connect with their audience in a way that was not possible before. This is an exciting development for the world of online content creation, and it will be interesting to see how the partnership evolves over time.

While these partnerships have been successful for Rumble.com, the company has also faced criticism for some of its collaborations. In particular, the company has been criticized for its association with controversial figures and media outlets, including Infowars and The Gateway Pundit.

Despite these criticisms, Rumble.com has continued to pursue its partnership strategy, emphasizing the importance of collaboration and mutual benefit. As the platform continues to grow and expand, it will be interesting to see what new partnerships and collaborations Rumble.com develops, and how they contribute to the platform's   success.

Rumble.com's Role in the Changing Media Landscape:
The Rise of Video and Social Media

In the current digital age, video and social media have transformed the way we consume and interact with content. Rumble.com has been a major player in this shift, pioneering a platform for video creators to share and monetize their content with a global audience.

As the popularity of video content has exploded in recent years, traditional media outlets have struggled to keep up with the demand for fresh and engaging content. Rumble.com has emerged as a key player in this space, offering a user-friendly platform that allows creators to share their work and build their brands.

At the heart of Rumble.com's success is its focus on user-generated content. By empowering creators with the tools they need to produce high-quality videos and reach a wider audience, the platform has helped to democratize the media landscape and shift power away from established media companies.

This shift has not been without its challenges, however. As the role of social media and user-generated content has grown, concerns have emerged over issues such as fake news, hate speech, and censorship. Rumble.com has taken a proactive approach to these issues, implementing strict policies and guidelines to ensure that its platform remains a safe and open space for all users.

As the media landscape continues to evolve, Rumble.com is well-positioned to play a leading role in shaping its future. By staying true to its mission of empowering creators and fostering free speech, the platform has the potential to shape the way we consume and interact with video content for years to come.

The Future of Rumble.com:
Innovations and New Frontiers

As Rumble.com continues to expand its reach and impact on the online video sharing space, the platform's future looks bright with a host of exciting innovations and new frontiers on the horizon. In this chapter, we will explore some of the most promising developments that Rumble.com is pursuing in order to remain at the forefront of the industry.

One major area of focus for Rumble.com is the ongoing evolution of its technology and infrastructure. The platform has invested heavily in improving its video encoding, storage, and delivery systems, resulting in faster load times, higher quality video, and a more seamless user experience. Rumble.com has also implemented cutting-edge machine learning algorithms and artificial intelligence tools to enhance its recommendation and curation capabilities, helping users discover the most relevant and engaging content on the platform.

Another key area of focus for Rumble.com is the expansion of its user base and the diversity of its content. The platform is actively seeking to attract a wider range of creators from around the world, with a particular emphasis on cultivating talent from underrepresented communities. Rumble.com is also exploring new content formats, such as short-form video and live streaming, to keep pace with changing user preferences and to offer more opportunities for creators to reach audiences.

In addition to its core video sharing features, Rumble.com is also exploring new ways to connect creators and audiences, such as through the development of a social media-like interface that will enable users to follow, share, and interact with their favorite content creators. The platform is also working on a range of tools and services to help creators monetize their content, including brand partnerships, merchandise sales, and paid subscriptions.

Looking even further ahead, Rumble.com is exploring the potential of emerging technologies such as virtual and augmented reality, which could offer entirely new ways for users to experience and interact with video content. The platform is also exploring the potential of blockchain and cryptocurrency technologies to create new revenue models and incentives for creators and users alike.

Rumble.com's future looks bright with a host of exciting new developments on the horizon. By continuing to invest in cutting-edge technology, cultivating a diverse and talented creator community, and exploring new content formats and revenue models, the platform is well positioned to remain a major player in the online video sharing space for years to come.

The Rumble.com Community:
User Stories and Feedback

Rumble.com owes much of its success to its community of users. While the platform has its own unique features, it's the content creators and viewers who truly bring it to life. In this chapter, we will explore the various ways in which the Rumble.com community has contributed to the growth of the platform, and how the company has responded to user feedback.

One of the main ways in which the Rumble.com community has made its mark on the platform is through the creation of a vast and diverse range of content. From humorous and lighthearted clips to hard-hitting news reports, there is no shortage of videos to be found on the site. This diversity is further enhanced by the fact that Rumble.com has users from all over the world, meaning that the platform is not limited to just one culture or language.

The Rumble.com community is also known for being passionate and engaged, often leaving comments and interacting with one another. This has created a sense of community on the platform, with users feeling like they are part of a larger group of like-minded individuals who share their interests and values.

Furthermore, Rumble.com has always been receptive to user feedback, and has used it to improve the platform over time. For example, the company has implemented changes to its algorithm and recommendations based on user behavior, making it easier for creators to get their content seen by a wider audience. Rumble.com has also made changes to its interface and monetization options, based on feedback from users who have found certain features difficult to use or understand.

In addition, Rumble.com has a dedicated team of community managers who work tirelessly to ensure that the platform remains a safe and positive space for all users. They review content to ensure that it complies with the company's policies and take action when necessary to remove content that violates those policies.

But it's not just the creators and viewers who have benefited from the Rumble.com community. The company has also shown its appreciation for its users through initiatives like the Rumble Rundown, a weekly newsletter that features the top videos and creators on the platform, as well as other news and updates. Rumble.com has also offered various contests and promotions, giving users the chance to win prizes and get their content seen by even more people.

Overall, the Rumble.com community is a vital and essential part of the platform. Without the passion and engagement of its users, the site would not be the thriving and dynamic video sharing platform that it is today. The company's willingness to listen to user feedback and make changes accordingly has only strengthened the bond between the platform and its users. It's clear that Rumble.com values its community, and the community, in turn, values the platform.

Rumble.com's Commitment to Free Speech and Democracy

Rumble.com has established itself as a platform that is committed to free speech and democracy. This commitment is rooted in the belief that the internet should be an open and free space where all voices can be heard, and where ideas can be exchanged without fear of censorship or reprisal. From its inception, Rumble.com has worked to create an environment where users are free to express themselves and engage with others on a wide range of topics and issues.

One of the key ways that Rumble.com has demonstrated its commitment to free speech is through its community guidelines. These guidelines outline the rules and expectations that users are expected to follow when using the platform, and they are designed to ensure that everyone can participate in a safe and respectful manner. Rumble.com has a zero-tolerance policy for hate speech, harassment, or any other form of content that is intended to harm or intimidate others. By setting clear standards for acceptable behavior, Rumble.com has been able to maintain a community that is both diverse and inclusive.

Rumble.com's commitment to free speech also extends to its approach to content moderation. Unlike some other social media platforms that have been criticized for their censorship practices, Rumble.com takes a hands-off approach to content moderation, only removing content that violates its community guidelines or is illegal under Canadian and US law. This means that users are free to express their opinions and ideas without fear of being silenced or having their content removed arbitrarily.

Another way that Rumble.com is working to promote free speech and democracy is by empowering content creators to monetize their content. Rumble.com's unique revenue sharing model allows creators to earn a share of the revenue generated by their content, giving them an incentive to create engaging and high-quality content that resonates with their audience. This model not only rewards creators for their hard work and creativity but also helps to ensure that a wide range of voices and perspectives are represented on the platform.

In addition to its commitment to free speech and democracy, Rumble.com has also been recognized for its efforts to promote media literacy and combat the spread of misinformation online. The platform has partnered with organizations such as NewsGuard, a company that provides ratings and reviews of news sources based on their reliability and credibility. This partnership allows Rumble.com users to easily identify trustworthy sources of information, helping to promote a more informed and engaged community.

Looking ahead, Rumble.com's commitment to free speech and democracy will continue to be a cornerstone of its mission. As the platform grows and evolves, it will undoubtedly face new challenges and opportunities, but its dedication to creating an open and inclusive space for all users will remain unchanged. Through its innovative approach to content creation, monetization, and community building, Rumble.com is poised to play a significant role in shaping the future of online discourse and democratic engagement.

Rumble.com and Political Discourse:
The Platform's Influence on Public Opinion

Rumble.com has become an increasingly popular platform for political discourse and news commentary, particularly in the United States. As traditional media outlets have become increasingly partisan, many individuals have turned to alternative sources for their news and analysis. Rumble.com has emerged as one of the most popular of these alternatives.

The platform's commitment to free speech has made it a natural home for conservative voices who feel marginalized by mainstream media outlets. However, Rumble.com is not limited to conservative content. It is an open platform that welcomes voices from across the political spectrum. In fact, the site's slogan is "Video for the people, by the people."

Rumble.com has provided a space for voices that are often shut out of mainstream media to share their opinions and ideas with a wider audience. This has led to the platform becoming a hub for a variety of perspectives, from the extreme right to the far left. The platform's algorithm does not prioritize any particular political viewpoint, but rather promotes videos that are getting the most engagement from viewers.

Many Rumble.com users see the platform as an important tool for promoting democracy and free speech. They argue that traditional media outlets are controlled by a small group of elites, and that alternative platforms like

Rumble.com are necessary to give a voice to the masses. The platform has become an important source of news and information for many people who are dissatisfied with mainstream media.

However, Rumble.com's influence on public opinion has not been without controversy. The platform has been accused of promoting extremist and false content, particularly during the 2020 U.S. presidential election. Some have also raised concerns about the platform's moderation policies, arguing that it is too permissive and allows hate speech and other harmful content to thrive.

Rumble.com has responded to these criticisms by reaffirming its commitment to free speech, but also by introducing new policies and measures to address harmful content. For example, the platform has recently introduced a system for content creators to flag videos that violate the platform's terms of service, and has hired additional moderators to review flagged content.

Rumble.com's role in political discourse and public opinion is a complex and evolving one. The platform's commitment to free speech and open dialogue is admirable, but it also creates challenges in terms of moderating harmful content. As Rumble.com continues to grow and expand, it will be interesting to see how it navigates these challenges and evolves to meet the needs of its diverse and passionate community of users.

The Rumble.com Brand:
Reputation, Marketing, and Public Image

As a relatively new player in the video-sharing industry, Rumble.com has quickly made a name for itself through its unique business model and its commitment to free speech. The Rumble.com brand has become synonymous with user-generated content, creative freedom, and democratic values. This chapter explores the company's reputation, marketing, and public image.

From the beginning, Rumble.com has positioned itself as an alternative to mainstream social media platforms that have been criticized for censorship and a lack of transparency. The company's commitment to free speech and its user-focused approach have resonated with a growing number of content creators and viewers who are looking for a platform where they can express themselves without fear of reprisal. Rumble.com's reputation as a defender of free speech has also made it a popular destination for political commentary, alternative news, and other forms of controversial content.

In terms of marketing, Rumble.com has focused on building a community of content creators and viewers who share the company's values. The platform's website and social media pages emphasize its mission to provide a space for people to share their stories and opinions freely. Rumble.com has also used influencer marketing to reach new audiences, partnering with popular YouTubers and other content creators who have migrated to the platform. In addition, the company has run ads on social media and other online channels to promote its brand and its unique features.

Rumble.com's public image has been shaped by a number of high-profile events and controversies. The platform's decision to host an alternative to YouTube's annual Rewind video was widely praised by content creators and viewers who were dissatisfied with the direction of YouTube's flagship program. However, Rumble.com has also faced criticism for its handling of certain types of content, particularly conspiracy theories and other forms of misinformation. The company has responded to these concerns by updating its policies and enforcing them more rigorously, while also acknowledging the need for continued improvement.

Looking to the future, Rumble.com will likely continue to face challenges as it grows and evolves. However, its commitment to free speech and user-generated content gives it a strong position in the market, and its reputation as a defender of democratic values will continue to be a key part of its brand identity. As the video-sharing industry continues to change, Rumble.com's focus on the needs and desires of its users will be a defining characteristic that sets it apart from its competitors.

The Legacy of Rumble.com:
A Lasting Impact on the Digital World

Since its inception in 2013, Rumble.com has become one of the most influential video sharing platforms on the internet. The platform's unique approach to content creation, monetization, and free speech has made it a formidable player in the online media landscape. With millions of users and an ever-expanding community, Rumble.com has left a lasting impact on the digital world.

One of the most significant ways that Rumble.com has influenced the digital world is by providing a space for creators to exercise their free speech rights. While other platforms have struggled to maintain a balance between free speech and community standards, Rumble.com has made it a priority to support the rights of its users to express their views. This commitment to free speech has not only contributed to the platform's popularity but has also set a standard for other social media and video sharing platforms to follow.

Another aspect of Rumble.com's legacy is its creator-focused monetization strategy. The platform's revenue model, which prioritizes the earnings of creators, has set it apart from other platforms that are accused of exploiting content creators. Rumble.com has made it possible for creators to earn a fair share of the revenue generated by their videos, thus encouraging a thriving community of content creators who can rely on the platform for their livelihood.

Rumble.com's impact can also be seen in the viral videos that have emerged from the platform. The platform's algorithm and recommendation engine have been instrumental in promoting videos that have gone on to become cultural phenomena. The success of these videos has not only brought more attention to the platform but has also created a new category of online entertainment that has captivated audiences around the world.

As Rumble.com continues to expand and evolve, it is likely to have an even greater impact on the digital world. Analysing their Financial Results for Q3 2022, they have reported their Monthly Active Uses of more the 70 Million, which was almost double of what they had 12 months prior. If they continue on this growth trajectory, they will reach a strong position to keep Rumble very relevant in the years to come.

With its commitment to free speech, creator monetization, and innovative technologies, the platform is poised to play a leading role in shaping the future of online media. As more users discover the platform's unique features, Rumble.com's legacy is sure to grow and continue to influence the digital world for years to come.

In September 2021, rumble.com went public in the Nasdaq stock exchange.
In a filing with the Securities and Exchange Commission, the founder Chris Pavlovski wrote:

"Rumble is creating the rails to a new infrastructure that will not be bullied by cancel culture. We are a movement that does not stifle, censor, or punish creativity and freedom of expression."

In conclusion, Rumble.com's legacy is defined by its commitment to free speech, creator monetization, and innovation. The platform has carved out a unique space in the online media landscape and has left a lasting impact on the digital world. As more users continue to discover the platform, it is clear that Rumble.com will remain a significant force in the years to come.

END